GOOGLE CLASSROOM:

A PROFESSIONAL TEACHER GUIDE TO TAKE YOUR CLASSROOM DIGITAL IN 2020. EVERYTHING YOU NEED TO KNOW ABOUT GOOGLE CLASSROOM APP + 50 STUDENT APPROACH IDEAS

MARTA SCHOLL

© **Copyright 2020 - All rights reserved.**

The content contained within this book may not be reproduced, duplicated or transmitted without direct written permission from the author or the publisher.

Under no circumstances will any blame or legal responsibility be held against the publisher, or author, for any damages, reparation, or monetary loss due to the information contained within this book. Either directly or indirectly.

Legal Notice: This book is copyright protected. This book is only for personal use. You cannot amend, distribute, sell, use, quote or paraphrase any part, or the content within this book, without the consent of the author or publisher.

Disclaimer Notice: Please note the information contained within this document is for educational and entertainment purposes only. All effort has been executed to present accurate, up to date, and reliable, complete information. No warranties of any kind are declared or implied. Readers acknowledge that the author is not engaging in the rendering of legal, financial, medical or professional advice. The content within this book has been derived from various sources. Please consult a licensed professional before attempting any techniques outlined in this book.

By reading this document, the reader agrees that under no circumstances is the author responsible for any losses, direct or indirect, which are incurred as a result of the use of information contained within this document, including, but not limited to, — errors, omissions, or inaccuracies.

TABLE OF CONTENTS

INTRODUCTION 3

CHAPTER 1. THE MODERN TEACHER 7

CHAPTER 2. PILLS OF MINDSET 10

CHAPTER 3. BENEFITS OF GOOGLE CLASSROOM 16

CHAPTER 4. DIFFERENCE BETWEEN GOOGLE CLASSROOM AND OTHERS PLATFORMS 24

CHAPTER 5. GETTING STARTED WITH GOOGLE CLASSROOM 30

CHAPTER 6. HOW TO USE GOOGLE CLASSROOM? 41

CHAPTER 7. USEFUL APPS FOR GOOGLE CLASSROOM 49

CHAPTER 8. STUDENT APPROACH IDEAS 63

CHAPTER 9. TIPS AND TRICKS TO GET THE MOST OUT OF GOOGLE CLASSROOM 73

CHAPTER 10. FAQS ABOUT GOOGLE CLASSROOM 81

CHAPTER 11. GUIDELINES & SUGGESTIONS FOR CLASSROOM MANAGEMENT AND INSTRUCTIONAL FORMS 85

CHAPTER 12. OTHER WAYS GOOGLE CLASSROOM CAN HELP YOU SUCCEED 92

CHAPTER 13. PROS AND CONS OF USING GOOGLE CLASSROOM IN ELEARNING 98

CONCLUSION 107

Introduction

Google Classroom is a web service that was developed by Google for educators and schools with the purpose of making assignments paperless and to streamline the file sharing system between students and teachers. Essentially, this uses the entire Google ecosystem, such as Google docs, slides and sheets for writing and presentation, the Gmail communication system, and for scheduling, you use Google calendar. Students can join the classes their teachers have made with the use of a private code, or are automatically imported from the domain. Every single class is separated based on folders within the drive, students can put work in there, and teachers can grade it. It essentially is like putting your entire classroom on a computer, and it does help streamline both the education, and the communication between the teachers, and the students alike.

The coolest part about this, is that if you don't want to talk on a computer or use a computer, there are mobile apps for both Android and Apple devices that lets students do assignments on their device, even put photos on there, share different apps and files, and also access information on their devices both online and offline. Even with this, teachers can contact and speak to students, they can monitor how a student is doing, and once they are graded, teachers can go back and add comments to their work on order to ensure that students have the best education possible.

Essentially, this has made teaching way more productive, it also allows teachers to manage the coursework that is there, and everything is in one place, providing a more meaningful collaboration between both of these parties, and ensuring that students get the help that they need when the going gets tough.

The system actually allows more administrative tasks to be done in an effective manner. Because of the G suite for education, it makes tasks that are otherwise boring much faster. It works wherever you are, teacher or student, whether it be from any computer, any mobile device, or whatever, and it allows teachers to have access to the assignments that are there, the course materials they need, and all of the feedback in one awesome place.

The coolest part about this is that it is free. It's free for schools that have signed up for G suite for education, and like with any of the tools the classroom meets one of the highest standards that's out there, and it's a super fun system, and it is free, and works better than most free software that's out there.

Another great thing about this, is that I t allows feedback to come back to the student right away. Educators are able to track the progress of a student, and let them know how they are doing. More focus can be put on making sure that the student gets it, which is something that many students want to have. The cool thing about this is how integrative this is to the workplace for students, and teachers will be able to help in a much timelier manner. Plus, it allows for a more personalized construction, and it will allow students to have a better time learning subjects as well.

For teachers and students, it will save them time, effort, paper, and it will allow teachers to create a better environment for assignments and quizzes, and you can always talk to parents and guardians with this. You can copy and tweak assignments as well one to another, and control multiple classes as well, which is great if you are looking to truly master this type of system. It is great for students and teachers alike, and allows for a collaborative system that will in turn create a better and more immersive system than you have thought possible.

Google Classroom employs the clean and easy to use user interface you see on all Google apps. Single design details enable users to understand and grasp how to use the app much easily and also enables the user to adapt to the app faster. The simple and intuitive interface can convert even the most least IT savvy of users.

Because it is a Google product, Classroom works seamlessly with other programs like Google Docs, Google Drive, Google Forms, and Google Calendar. This greatly expands your options for how you interact with your students using programs you're all already familiar with.

Google is also very conscious as a company about internet security. They do not use any information from Google Classroom for advertising purposes, and make sure it's completely secure so no one else can, either. This protects the privacy of both students and teachers who use the interface.

Digital classrooms in general also have some distinct advantages over traditional set-ups. If you're still not sure how Google Classroom could be useful for you, reading through some of the ways it can be helpful for teachers may just sway you toward giving it a try.

Chapter 1 The Modern Teacher

One of the first questions that you may have about Google Classroom is what this platform is going to be able to do with this. There are quite a few different platforms that are similar to this one so you may be curious as to how this one is going to be the best option for you compared to the other ones. Not only are you going to get some of the great features that come with Google and what you are familiar with, which is one of the main benefits that you will see when working in Google Classroom.

Luckily, there are quite a few different things that you will be able to work with when working in Google Classroom. Some of the things that Google Classroom will be able to help you do include:

• Using Gmail at school. As a teacher, you will be able to create your own Gmail account. From there, you can search for any important messages or ones that are school related. You won't have to worry about the ads or any other delays that are common with some of the other email services. Gmail is one that many people are familiar with so you will be happy to use this more often.

• As a teacher, you will find that working with Google Classroom is going to help you to streamline your class. You will be able to do this by creating your assignments, being able to share your assignments and announcements with ease, and you can even grade them without wasting a lot of time.

- It is easy for both the teachers and the students to work together through docs. You will be able to create as well as edit various presentations, docs, and spreadsheets inside of your browser. In addition, you are able to do all of this while making sure that all of the changes are saved automatically. It is also possible for more than one person to work on something at the same time without having any issues.

- Your students will be able to share their work, as well as save their work, all on the cloud. This makes it easier for them to access the files whenever they want, even if they are not at home. This can be helpful for you as the teacher as well because you can upload some information to the cloud as well for your students to get ahold of. This helps save some of the hassle and the time that comes with sending attachments or merging together the different versions.

- The Google Calendar is a great option to use with the Google Classroom. Calendars in here are able to be shared. This makes it easier to plan for projects and you can also integrate together with your hangouts, contacts, email accounts, and Google Drive.

- As the teacher, you are going to find that using Google Calendars can be great. You can put up an announcement or an assignment and give it a due date. Then this due date and assignment are going to show up on the class page for all of the students that are linked to this classroom. You won't have to constantly update students about when a due date is about to come. They just need to take a look at their own Calendar to find out this information.

- If you feel that you need to set up a website that you are able to use for your class, Google Classroom is able to help out. This is something that you could do for a specific project or event or you can set it up so that the students are able to create some of their own websites as well.

- If it is needed, you are able to conduct meetings that are face to face with the help of video calls to your students. This can be really efficient if a student has a quick question that they would like to have answered. Some teachers have been able to use this service in order to create their own virtual field trip.

- Sometimes the chats and the emails can get all over the place and there are going to be too many of them. The teacher is able to archive these emails and these chats so that they can go through them at a later time if you would like. It is also really easy to organize your emails and chats so it is easier for you to use.

- It is possible to use some of the different add-on apps that you need to make more happen within the class. You could use Google+, Blogger, and Google Groups to make the class a bit more productive than you can in a traditional classroom.

These are just a few of the things that you are able to do when working within Google Classroom. As the teacher, you are able to pick out the things that you want to do inside the classroom, and each class is going to be a little bit different. It is completely fine to mix and match things together to make them personalized for the class that you are teaching.

Chapter 2 Pills Of Mindset

Google Classroom was built for both the educator and learner in mind. It isn't only the teachers who can do so many things with Google Classroom, but students can also harness the full capabilities of this application. Student's reaction to Google Classroom is whenever the teacher, who is the main Manager of the Classroom, uploads content in the Classroom.

Here are some of the various things that students can do with Google Classroom.

Change Ownership

When you turn in an assignment, the teacher becomes the owner of your document. You are no longer the owner, and therefore you are unable to edit the text. Turned in the wrong assignment? Simply click on the 'Unsubmit' button. You would need to refresh Google Classroom once you un-submit so that you can resend a new document.

Assignment listings

Students can find a list of all the assignments created by teachers by clicking on the menu icon located at the top left-hand corner of Google Classroom. Practically all assignments that have not been archived can be viewed in this list.

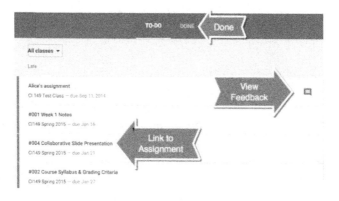

Utilize the Mobile App for easier access

We know students are always on their mobile phone. One of the best ways to get notified if you have a new assignment is through the Google Classroom's mobile app. The mobile app can be downloaded and installed from the Playstore or iTunes. The app allows students to view their assignments and submit their work directly from the app. This mainly works when students are requested to submit real life samples, or a video or a combination of photos. All they need to do is take pictures of their samples or their solutions and then upload it to the Google Classroom.

No worries if you haven't clicked on Save

Encourage your students to use Google Docs to do their assignments. If you have given work that requires them to write reports, write a story or anything that requires their use of a Word document, use Google Docs because it saves edits automatically. This eliminates your student's excuses of not being able to complete their homework because they did not save it. Also, it just makes things easier when you are so engrossed with completing your work, you forget to save; Google Docs does it for you.

Sharing isn't the same thing as turning in

When a student clicks open an assignment to hand in their assignment, they need to click on TURN IN. Sharing an assignment to the Google Classroom is not the same thing as turning in your completed work. Make sure you click on TURN IN to submit your assignment in due time.

You will not lose assignments

Unless you delete it. Any documents you upload to your Google Classroom is only seen between you and the teacher. Any assignments you upload to your Google Drive will be seen on the teachers Google Drive as well. Your Google Drive is the storage system for Google Classroom and it works the same way for both the teacher as well as the students.

Due Dates

You'd have a harder time explaining to your teacher why you have not submitted your assignment especially since the due dates are continuously shown on an assignment. Assignments that are not due yet are indicated on the class tile on the home page as well as the left of the page late assignments have a particular folder, where the teacher can accurately see the assignments listing from the menu icon on the upper left of the page.

> **UPCOMING ASSIGNMENTS**
>
> DUE MAR 6
>
> #016 Collaborative Presentation

Returning an Assignment

Students working on a Google Document can return at any time to the file that they are working on. Get back to the assignment stream and click on Open and it will take you to a link to the documents that you have on Google Drive. Click on the document and get back right into it. You can also access this file directly from your personal Google Drive. It is the same way you click on any document on your desktop to work on it again. Plus side is Google Docs auto saves.

Communicating with teachers

It's either you communicate publicly on Google Classrooms for the entire class to see, or you communicate privately. Communicating privately helps a lot especially for students who are shy and prefer to speak to the teacher directly without the involvement of other classmates. It also helps the teacher speak privately to address a student's issue on an assignment without making them feel inadequate or that they have not done well.

Commenting on Assignments

Comments on an assignment are viewable by your classmates on Google Classroom when it is made on any assignments uploaded to the app. Students just need to click on 'Add Comments' under an assignment. If students would like to communicate in private, with you, they can leave it on the assignment submission page. Within a specific document, you can use the File Menu and click on 'Email collaborators' to message or link a document to the teacher.

Add Additional files to an assignment

Students and teachers can both add additional files to an assignment. For students, they can add in files that did not come together with a template the teacher gave. You can click on ADD additional files on the assignment submission page again. Links from websites can also be added. Additional files help in the attempt to provide a wholesome blended learning approach in schools because you can add files of different formats and types.

Chapter 3 Benefits Of Google Classroom

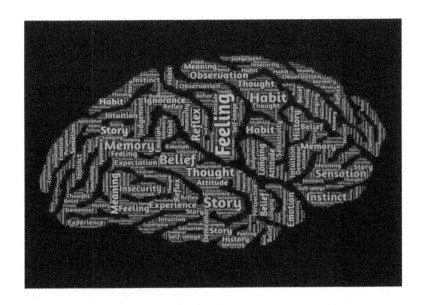

So what is so great about Google Classroom for both teachers and students? Well, read on to find out. Google Classroom is great for both educators, and for students, and it ultimately does make it easier for teachers to do their job. Some teachers may be against the technological changes, but there are many benefits to this.

Better Accessibility

Google Classroom can be accessed from any device that uses Google chrome, regardless of platform. This means, you can work on your assignments on an iPad, or even on a mobile phone, and they're uploaded to Google drive and the classroom folder, meaning they can be used wherever, whenever, and students never have to worry about losing their assignments anymore, that's for sure!

Saves Paper!

Google Classroom is completely paperless, so you won't have to worry about printing thirty-plus copies for students that have a knack for losing their papers, nor do you have to worry about students misplacing paper well, it's all online. All of the assignments are uploaded there, and once there, they're saved to the drive, which means that students can complete the assignments there, send it, and it's saved to drive, and even if they don't save it, it's there so you never have to worry about students using the "my computer crashed" excuse for the third time.

Exposes both Teachers and Students to Online Learning

Since it's all online, Google Classroom allows for students to work in an online environment, which is something that students will soon learn about the moment they go to college. If you want a master's degree in education, you need to actually do some of your work online. The same goes for many majors, but many students don't know how to navigate an online class. Well, Google Classroom is a great way to actually understand how to work in an online environment, and by being exposed to it early on, it allows for them to not be as shell-shocked when they finally make their way to college and realize that they'll have a lot of classes similar to this in the future.

Super easy to Get Materials

It's also super easy to access the materials, but this is good because no matter where they end up, they'll get the materials. Students that are absent can get the classroom materials from home if needed by simply logging in and getting the assignments by clicking on this. Gone are the days of having to deal with students having to chase after you just to get assignments.

All Work is There

One thing that's super annoying and frustrating for teachers is the fact that some students have a knack for losing work. Well, Google Classroom nips that in the bud. How? Well, it takes out that external document, and instead everyone works in Google drive. Google drive saves everything immediately, regardless of if you make one change to add a word, or if you work on the assignment for hours on end. It's super nice, and it saves you a lot of headaches. It's all there, and students never have to worry about "accidentally" losing work.

Creates Collaborative Learning

Because everything is digitally, you can share content with peers in one singular document that can be edited together, and then share another version for the students without the editing to this. If you want to, you can create assignment worksheets that are different for teachers and students, and from there, drive together a question and answer system, and even create deeper discussions. It allows for teachers to really engage with students. With the way technology is bringing everyone together, it's no wonder why teachers want to integrate this further and further into the classroom.

Instant Feedback and Analysis

Gone are the days of having to wait for whether or not you did well on a quiz, or if you will get enough answers. Teachers don't have to sit around and meticulously spend a ton of time grading assignments. Instead, you can deliver quizzes that have automatic answers, or even give a detailed report on what teachers can do better. You can help those who answered questions incorrectly add more to this, which is super nice, and it is super easy to integrate into the system. Students will get their answers faster, and teachers can grade everything in a more detailed way.

Saves you a Ton of Time

For students, this saves them a ton of time trying to save various documents, hoping that it gets to their drive, or even just working on paper and awkwardly turning it in. It also saves them time on answering questions, because let's be honest, a day could go by and they may not get the answer right away. By utilizing Google Classroom, you can save yourself. a boatload of time, and ultimately participate way more in this as well.

Communication Success!

Google Classroom saves you a ton of time when it comes to communicating. If a student has a question, they can send an email, comment on an assignment stream, send comments privately, or even provide feedback on something. Teachers can do the same, and the teachers can as well send specific emails to communicate with students that have a specific issue, or who need a lot more help. That way, they won't fall behind. It is making a difference in terms of how students handle the workload, and teachers can also follow the different standards, and in truth, it makes it so much easier for everyone.

Students Take Ownership

One thing that teachers try to help students get better at, is trying to stay more engaged in their studies. Well, Google Classroom can help with this. It is not just students reading and commenting on answers that the other students may have, it is also being in charge of their homework. Students can learn a subject they're having trouble with a little bit better if they are struggling with it, and in turn, if they want to utilize additional resources on their won, they can. The best part of Google Classroom is really just hos students can take charge of their learning environment, and in turn, create the best learning experience that they can.

In-Depth Data Analysis

If you want to see whether or not students understand, and any areas they may be stumbling on, this is how.

You can even take the grades and export them from google sheets, or just keep everything there. If you want to analyze and sort them as well, in order to see how students are faring and where you need to focus, you can use this as a super helpful resource tool.

Lots of times, you can see trends in grades, and if you notice there is something wrong with a student's learning, you can take the information that's there, and from there, use this to help students get a better idea of what is going on.

Teachers can get more involved with the use of google classroom, and they can see just where their students need some help, and any other resources that can assist them as well to be successful.

Good Security

Security is actually very strong on this. If you have an IT team, they can control the passwords so if a student does forget, they can fix it quickly. With the API that is there, everything is synched up, so the teachers can have everything put together. It's also got a high-level security, which means that you won't have to worry about any breaches and the like, for it's also quite easy to work with.

See that Real-Time Progress

Are you sick of trying to have to walk around and see whether students are working on this, or maybe you want to help students if they are going in the wrong direction? Well, now you can with this. With the Google Classroom system, you can press Student Work, and you can look at the thumbnail of every single student in order to see their progress in real-time, so you can track and see if there are any problems if you are looking to change this. You can also use the revision history feature to look at changes that have happened, allowing you to see what worked, or what didn't work, and how you can fix that.

Chapter 4 Difference Between Google Classroom And Others Platforms

Let's talk about Google Classroom versus Apple classroom. Google Classroom is the focus of this book, but how does it stack up to Apple classroom? Well, read on to find out.

The Hardware difference

The biggest difference that you'll run into is the hardware elements. Apple classroom is free for iPad, and essentially, the classroom involves using multiple different iPad, and the teachers will put these on the device, allowing students to use these as an integrative tool. The teacher iPad is essentially a collection of these powers, in order to give a learning experience. Essentially, it's similar to Google Classroom, and once this is configured, it's connected to devices, and the iPad are shared, and once the session is done, it can be signed out of. It's a way to keep students focused, shows students different screens, and it can share documents with the class through the use of AirDrop. It also shows student work on Apple TV, reset the passwords for students, and it also can create groups of students based on the apps that they use, and it allows teachers to create groups and teams. Basically, it's a way to have Apple within the classroom, and through the use of the iPad, it's more collaborative directly within the direct learning atmosphere.

Good for lower Level Grades

Now, you'll notice immediately, that the only similarity is that they both have the word "classroom" in there. This means, that Apple classroom is more of a direct classroom tool, and it helps teachers show apps and pages to students that might have trouble with this, and show off the work that's there. Teachers in upper grades benefit from this because it monitors the activity, but the thing is, the student can find out if the teacher is watching very fast. It's more of a direct device to use for learning within the classroom, whereas with Google Classroom, it focuses on both in and outside of the classroom.

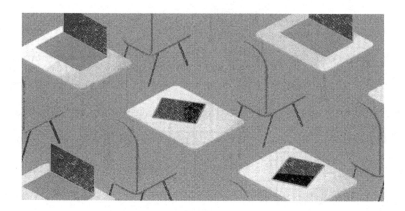

Google Classroom focuses on organization

One big part of Google Classroom, is the organization element. It is all collaborated with Google drive, which essentially means that learning based on connections and education is there based on organization than directly into the classroom. Google Classroom makes it easy for teachers to assign the work, and allows students to have better organization on assignments and allows them to get updates faster. It also allows it to go paperless too, which is a big plus. Google Classroom focuses on showing work that needs to be done, any grades that they have, and any assignments that they missed. It's more of a tool to better organization of the student body over everything else.

Apple Classroom Has more interactive Lessons

For those teachers that want to have a more engaging class, and that's where Apple Classroom may work better. For example, if you're teaching a younger crowd, it may be better to have Apple classroom, because let's face it, do first graders really need to navigate Google drive and submit documents? Course not. They would benefit more from Apple classroom, since it involves showing the app, and allows teachers to teach, and students to focus on what the teacher is teaching. It's focused as well on interacting with the student, and it shows the assignment that they work on, giving teachers a chance to look at each of the pieces of work that the student does, and the most recently used options. There even the screen view that shows the iPad, and it is a good way to keep direct focus on the students within the classroom.

So if you're a more interactive-lesson focused teacher, such as you're teaching students the colors, or want students to not screw around in class, the Apple Classroom device may be a better option for you. If you're a teacher who is more interested in having essays, homework, and other elements easily organized in one place, then yes, Google Classroom may be more your style.

Google Classroom allows for Multiple Devices to Be Used

Now, you can get the tablets for Google Classroom, but if you want to have students work on something right away, they totally can. The beauty of Google Classroom, is that it's not attached to a brand. You can get Google on your computers, and installing chrome is super easy. With that, you are given way more options on using this. Google Classroom can be downloaded as an app too on our device, meaning that if you've got a phone, tablet, or whatever, you're essentially free to use this with whatever you want. That's what's so nice about it, because students can work on assignments right away, and from there, submit it to the teacher. It also allows for students to work on different subjects while on the go, and can share different questions and resources with the teacher. It is much more interactive, and is perfect for if you have a classroom with multiple smart devices.

The problem with Apple, is that it's a brand. you're essentially working only with Apple brand, meaning that it's highly limited. After all, not everyone may have a Mac, or an iPad, so it doesn't really have as much use as say Google Classroom does.

You don't Have to Choose

The reality of this though, is that there are some key differences, and you can choose based on needs, with Apple classroom being more of a focus directly within the class environment itself, and Google classroom being more on workflow and assignments. They're two different tools, but comparing it is like Apples and oranges, which is a bit different from your average device comparison, since it's often pitted against each other in the technology realm. The truth is, you shouldn't have to choose between both of them, because some teachers benefit from both. If you really want to make your classroom the best it can be, sometimes the best answer is to add both of these services, since they're both really good at what they do, and they complement each other well. The answer is, you shouldn't choose one or the other. If you want to get both, get both. If the district can handle both, get both. But, if you're a teacher for a younger group of students, Apple classroom works. If you're a teacher for older students, Google Classroom works.

Apple classroom and Google Classroom are two very different types of software, but both of them accomplish the goal of helping children learn better, so that they can use these skills to better their life now, and in their future learning endeavors and studies that they will embark on.

Chapter 5 Getting Started with Google Classroom

Now, Google classroom has lots of benefits to it. We will tell you what you can get out of this as a teacher, and how you can start with creating plans on this.

What Teachers and Students can Do with This?

What teachers can do with this is actually quite awesome. If you've ever wanted to manage a class directly without any problems, or even just ditching the paperwork, then this is the way to go.

In this, you can do the following, but of course it's not just limited to this:

- Create classes

- Manage classes

- Put together some amazing assignments, even using extensions

- Grade everything right in one place

- Give feedback on everything that you provide to students

- Help those as needed

- Add some extra learning extensions to help with improving your understanding of this system.

For students, you can do virtually the same thing that teachers can do, but on the student end:

- Get your grades from the teacher

- Get help on a subject as needed

- Turn in assignments, which essentially helps ditch the paper and minimizes excuses

- Talk to other students through the stream or email, which helps out a lot if you're struggling with classes

- Keep track of all of the materials and coursework all in one place

This is awesome software for students because it puts everything all in one place, and it does help students with keeping everything in order

How to Get Started

Now you know what this does for teachers and students, but how do you get started? Well, what you need t do, is first make sure that you have an existing Google account. If that's not already done, then you'll need to make that. It's quite simple, and it's really just your email and password. Then, you want to choose the option to go to classroom.Google.com account. For teachers, once you do this, you'll sign in, and then you'll get a handy welcome screen. From there, you'll then be able to create a class, and we will discuss how you create, manage them, and even how to remove them in the next section.

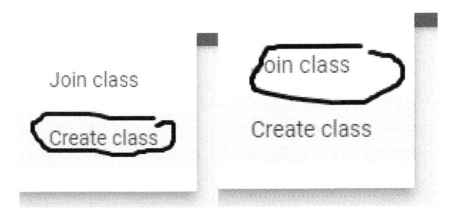

By understanding how to use this, and the importance of this for teachers, and how you essentially get started, you'll be well on your way

to using Google Classroom with everything, and it'll make everything all the more easier.

How to Create and Manage a Class

Classes are fun to create, organize and manage the class, and how you can remove classes once they are done. Classes are the most important aspect of this, since it's where everyone will be, and if you know how to put all of this together, you'll be well on your way to a successful result with Google Classroom.

How to create a Class

now, once you've logged in and everything, it's time to create a class. When you first do log in, you get the option of either student, or teacher. Always make sure that you indicate that you are a teacher, and if you mess up, you need to contact the administrator to reset this. It's super important, because students are limited in their options compared to teachers, and it can be quite frustrating. Now, if you're a student, you simply press when you get the plus button to join a class. For teachers, it's create a class.

Now, if you've already got classes, chances are you'll see some other names there. They'll be displayed on the screen itself, but every time you press the plus button, you'll then be able to add more to this.

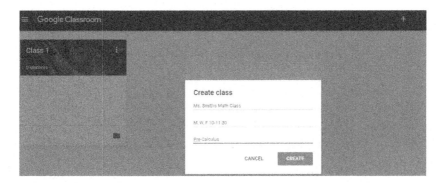

Next, you're given a class dialogue boss. you'll then type in the name, and the section of this. you'll be able to immediately create the class from here.

But, if you want to add more to it, you can go to the about tab, choose the title of the course, along with the description of this, the location of this, and even add materials here. You do need to have a name for the class itself, since this is how students will find the class when they open it up. If you have classes with multiple names on it, you'll definitely want to specify, either via time or day, especially if you've got a lot of sections. The section field is how you do this, and you can create a subject as well, based on the list of subjects they provide for you.

Some teachers like to make these very descriptive, and you should ideally add as much information as you feel that you need for this. But do remember, that you make sure that it isn't some wall of text that students will read and get confused. As a teacher, you should make sure that you do this in a way where students will get the information easily, and that they'll be able to delineate each class. It's also important to make it easy for your own benefit.

How to manage a Class

First thing that you can do when changing the class and managing it, is giving it a theme. One thing that you'll notice is that you don't have students in there once it's created, so you can have a bit of fun with this. One way you can do it, is on the right side near the header of the general class, is you need to change the class theme. You can use the themes that are there to be offered. Some photos of classes themselves are good options, and you can use different templates for each one so that you know exactly what class you're using, because themes can sometimes be a bit complicated.

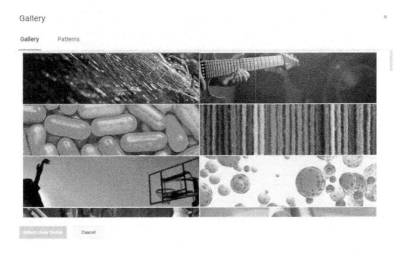

How to Remove, Delete, and View a Class

When using Google Classroom, sometimes you'll want to delete a class when it's the end of the semester, and you can always restore it as needed if you need it. You can also delete it if you never want to see the class again, or have no use for it because you've got the assignments already. Now, if you don't achieve these, they stick around, so make sure that you achieve them.

Now archived classes essentially means that they're in an area where you have the materials, the work students have, and the posts. You can view it, but you can't actually use it, and is good if a student wants the materials.

Archiving classes is simple to do. You choose the class, see the three dots, press, it and then, it's archived.

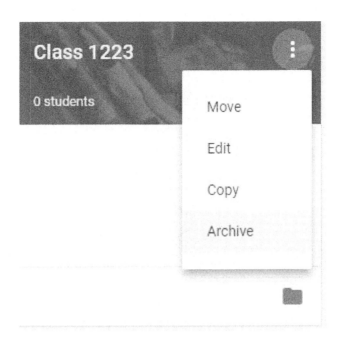

Now to view an archived class after it's been archived, you press the three line menu, go down to the tab that says achieve classes, and then choose the class you want to see.

To delete a class though, you essentially want to do the same thing. Remember, that you need to achieve the class before you can delete it, so scroll all the way down, choose achieve classes, and from there, once you have the classes, you want to press the three dots option, and then choose to delete this. From there, you'll have the class fully removed. Remember though, you can't undo this once you've done this, and if you do choose to delete a class, you don't have access to the comments or the posts, but if you have any files that are in the drive, you can always access those, since you have those in the class files themselves.

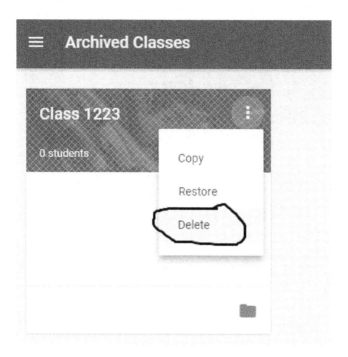

Other Tips and Tricks for class Management

There are a few class management things that you can implement, and some tips and tricks that go into Google Classroom. The first thing that happens, is that when you get to the classes tab on there, and you want to drag and move the classes around, you could do so. This is a good way to change the order of this, and it's quite easy to do.

Another important thing to remember too, is that you have the classroom function. It's quite nice, and if you want to change the calendar or view it, you essentially can press the icon with the calendar that's on there, and you can even check it out to see what's coming up for every single class, because some classes may do certain things at different times of the semester.

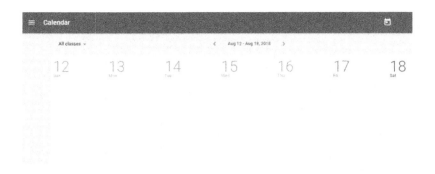

Finally, you can always adjust the settings at any point. This is done with the gear that you see on the home screen. Here, you can change the name of the class, especially if it's confusing, show the class code if you need it, and also decide on the stream and also to showcase whether or not you want items to be deleted or displayed. There are other features there too, and it's all right there waiting for you to be used.

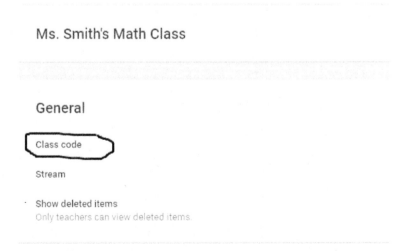

When it comes to Google Classroom, knowing how to create the classes is a big part of it. If you have classes that you want to add, or you want to get started with Google Classroom, this is the way to go, and it's the surefire way to success with this.

Chapter 6 How To Use Google Classroom?

Adding in a class

In order to add one of your first classes in Google Classroom, you would use the following steps if working inside of a web browser:

• Go to classroom.google.com and then sign in with your credentials.

• Click on the (+) sign, and then on Create Class.

• Look around to see the first empty text box and then place in the name that you would like to name the class.

• Under the name of the class, you will want to add in a short description. There should be a second text box for you to be able to do this. You can also add in the section, the grade level, or the class time to make it easier to find the class.

• When all of this is set up, you will just need to click on the create button to get the class started.

The steps above are all about working on a web browser on your personal computer. If you would like to use your iOS device to set up the class, you would use the following steps.

• Go to your classroom.google.com account and then click on the icon that kind of looks like a person.

- From here, you can click on, or use your fingers, the (+) sign and then click on Create Class.

- From here you will need to add in the information for the class that you are working on. You can enter the name of the class as well as a small description of the class in your second box.

- When all of the right information is inside of the boxes, you can click on Create and your class is ready.

You can also choose to set up one of these classrooms with the help of your Android device. Some of the steps that you can take to use your Android device includes:

- Go to the classroom.google.com and use your credentials in order to sign in.

- Look for the icon that looks like a person and click on that to start.

- Touch on the (+) sign and then push Create Class.

- Enter the name of the class as well as the description and the other information that you would like to use in the second box.

- When all of this is in the right place, you can click on create and then your class is all ready to go.

Adding in a Resource Page to the Class

- Go to your classroom.google.com page.

- Choose the class that you want to use in order to add in a resource page if you have more than one class.

- From here you will click on the About button on the top of the page.

- You can then pick out a title and a description for your class from here.

- In the Room Field, add in a location and then leave it blank.

- Click on Add Materials to add the different resources that you want to use in the classroom. For example, if the teacher wants to attach a specific file, they will be able to click on the right icon. Then they can locate the item that they want to use and click on Add. If you don't need to add on an attachment, just click on X.

- Once all of the attachments are placed in the resource page you can click on Post, and then make sure to save as well.

Add in other teachers

- Go in and sign in to your classroom.google.com account.

- You can then go and pick out the class that you would like to add in another teacher or two to, and then click on the About button that is on the top of the screen.

- Here you should see a button that says Invite Teacher. Click on that and then put a check mark into the box that is next to the teachers you would like to invite. They will already need to be in the Google Classroom system for your institution for you to be able to do this.

- If you decide to add in everyone who is on the list, you are able to click on Select All to make this happen.

- If you notice that one of the teachers that you would like to invite is not on this list, you will just need to click on My Contacts and then follow the steps above again.

Inviting in the students

Go to your classroom.google.com account.

From here, you will want to work on adding the students to the class that you have chosen. So go into the chosen class and then click on Students and then Invite.

- Tick on the box next to all of the names of the students that you need to add into the class. If all of the students on the list need to be invited you can click on Select All.

- If you need to see some other lists to get the students that you would like to add in, you would need to click on My Contacts. You can also click on Directory to see some of the other students who are in your domain.

- When your list is all done, you are able to click on Invite students.

This is going to send out an invite to all of your students. They will be able to click on the link and then be added to the Classroom that you set up. You can also choose to give your students a code. You would come up with a code for the class and then the students will be able to go in and add themselves to the class. Some of the steps that you would need to do to give out the code to the classroom include:

- Go to your classroom.google.com account.

- From here, you will need to get into the class page at the bottom of the stream. Here you should be able to find the email addresses for the students here.

- Send out an email to all of the students from there with the code inside so that they can use this to join the class. You can also choose to write down the code and give it to the students in class.

- You will want to let the students know that they will be able to sign into the classroom by visiting classroom.google.com and then click on the (+) sign before entering the code that you give them and pressing on Join.

- You will then be able to disable or reset the code as you need.

At this point, the students should be able to get into your classroom and see the information that you put there. You can also choose to invite students that are on a particular Google Group. The steps that you would need to make this happen include:

- Go to your classroom.google.com account.

- You can add in the students that you want with the class and then click on the Students button on the top.

- From here you will want to click on Students, then Invite, and then My Contact.

- You can then select the particular Google Group that you would like to use in order to invite people from.

- Here you can add a tick to the box that is next to the name of the student that you need to add to this class. You can also choose to click on Select All if it is easier for you and you want to add in all of the students.

- When that is done, you can click on Invite Students and the invitation will be sent out.

Setting the permissions for the class

- Go into the Classroom page for the class you are working on and click on Students.

- From here you can click on Students can Post and Comment. You can then tweak how this works, but there are a few things that you should keep in mind:

    o   Students can post and comment: if you click on this one, it means that the students are able to make posts as well as comments when they would like. If you are choosing this one, you should make sure to set out some ground rules for what is allowed with posting to keep things in order.

    o   Students can comment only: this means that the student will be able to add in the comments that they want, but they are not able to start their own posts. If you are working on a discussion question, you are able to just have the students comment if that is easier.

    o   Only the teacher can post or comment: this means that you do not want to allow the students to post or comment on this in any way. This is usually not one that you would want to use since Google Classroom works the best when you are able to communicate with each other.

Removing a Student or a Teacher

- Click on the About part of the classroom that you are in. You can then look for the name of the teacher before clicking on Remove From Class.

- To work with the students, you would need to click on the Students Tab. Look through this to find the name of the student that you would like to remove.

- From here, click on Actions and then click Remove.

- You will need to click on Remove again to confirm that you would like to remove the student.

Viewing the Class Calendar

- Click on Calendar when you are in the Classroom page.

- Then you can click on an assignment that is on your Calendar, or you can click on Quick Question in order to access the information from the Student page if needed.

- You can click on the arrow next to know what is going on or this week or even the following week so you can plan out your time.

- If you would like to be able to filter out the events, you can click on the All Classes button, and then choose which class you need to have a filter of events for.

Chapter 7 Useful Apps For Google Classroom

Math Apps

Here are some math apps that should be included to better your experience:

The first is Motion Math. This is an innovative tool that teaches foundations for math, with some interactive visuals. With this, you can integrate it into your lesson plan. Students can do these problems at the pace that they like, and you as a teacher just have to make sure that you have them doing it. It is good for grades K-6, and it can give instructions on how to solve problems with context, and it does measure the learning of students with a growth mindset, and allows for visuals to be used to understand math.

Quick Math Pack is a bundle of four different apps that allow for some quick learning opportunities for a student. These are for grades K-5 as well, and it goes over basic math concepts, fractions, and also telling time. For four bucks, you can have this app bundle, and they're great for students who want some extra practice with learning various math concepts. It also comes with a handwriting software, allowing the student. To write it onto the interface to better remember math concepts.

Apollonius is a geometry app for students who want to learn basic geometry. It's used to help showcase various constructions that are made, and it can be made with both a compass and a ruler, using this to explore the different kinds of objects that you can make. It is used with touchscreen devices, so that you can get the best experience that you can with this app. It's good for learning basic shapes too, and for some, it can help you better understand how angles and lines interact with one another.

Mathspace is a computer-based math system that allows students to have problems fully worked out, and get instant feedback and help. It contains over 70,000 different questions, ranging from algebra, graphing, geometry, statistics, and geometry. You can use this for students anywhere from grades 6-12, meaning that it's a great app for those older students. It's also got math writing recognizing software, where it will recognize the items that are written, and correct them on the spot, giving you hands-on help for bettering your understanding of difficult concepts. This is usually where students tend to fall behind in math, and this software can prevent that from happening accordingly.

Assorted VR Apps

VR is super popular these days, to the point where Google Classroom has a couple apps on it itself. But, here are the best apps to use relating to VR.

Animal flashcards is a great way to use AR with flashcards, allowing children to learn about various animals and also learn the letters easier. It's a unique app, and you get realistic rendered animals to look at. You can tap the image to hear the name, and the letters that are in the name of the animal.

Quiver is coloring but made for learning. It's AR coloring, which means that you can color some interesting characters with this technology, view cool animals, play interactive games, and even get quizzes and facts on it. You can learn about many different animals and other factors with this fun app, and it certainly allows you to explore your own personal artistic side as well.

Quiver

Boulevard is an art teacher's dream. With this, you essentially get the VR and AR experience of going to different museums, to look at the works that are there. Sure, you may not be able to take your class to the British museum, but this app allows you to explore this experience, and if you're an art teacher who wants to work on art history, or even a history teacher that dabbles in art, this is for you.

Skill Building Apps

Khan academy is one that allows you to get video explanations on anything, from math, economics, history, and more, and it comes with interactive practices, related to common core, and other learning tools that allow you to help improve with learning, and you can flex your muscles by understanding different concepts. It's also set to help with standardized tests too, which makes it even better, and a very good app for general skill building.

SentenceBuilder is a great app for those who want to get better at building and creating sentences. For those who want to get better at grammar, this is for you. With this, it will allow children in elementary school to build sentences and concepts, and it mostly focuses on bettering ones understanding of connecting words, which is a focal part and a problem that many who try to understand the English language. There are pictures to make sentences with, and it does use reinforcement to correct this, and teachers can even track the progress of students as well.

For students who need a bit of help organizing their lives and homework, Studious is the answer for this. It's a homework planner that allows students to organize and improve their ability to keep track of everything. you'll get reminders of when assignments are due, when tests are coming up, and you can even take notes and send emails. It is great, because you can scan and print documents from your phone, create a personal assignment calendar, organize your assignments to be prepared, and allow you to edit your courses and such, giving you a chance to improve your ability to understand classes.

American wordspeller is great for those who want to better their own understanding of words, learn how to spell them correctly, and allows you to type it in how it sounds to you. It's a way to understand how some words are spelled, and it can help you to better understand the English language. English can be hard, since there are so many different words out there, but this can help you understand the word meaning, and help to prevent you from getting confused about certain words that are out there, such as how carrot/karat/carat all sound the same.

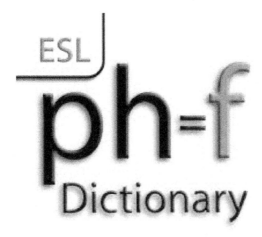

Stack the countries is a great app to help you learn where countries are, and it's good if you're in a geography or social studies class. In this, you literally get a map, with some animated little countries, and from there, you literally drop them wherever you want. You want to build and stack all of these countries correctly to help you win levels. It allows you to better understand the locations of different places, and you can even choose to focus on a continent, or even the entire world, and it even comes with flash cards to help you brush up on your geography as well.

Finally, we've got Evernote. It essentially is a great app for organizing your notes, and your life. You can hand write notes on a device, save them, and then organize them. For those who don't like to use the handouts, or like to take their own notes and the teacher doesn't provide notes, this is great. Plus, it allows you to have a better understanding of all your notes, in order to make your learning experience so much better.

With all of these apps, you'll see here that Google classroom can work with many different apps to make it better. While yes, some are paid, others are free, and you as a student, or even as a teacher, can benefit from all of these. Using these can make your experience worthwhile, and can help you become a better learner.

Chapter 8 Student Approach Ideas

Teaching Math

If you are thinking how else you can expand the experience of learning math or using Classroom in your math classes, here are some creative ways to build on.

1. Problem of the Week

Aptly known as POW, POWs can be anything that you feel needs more attention. It can be a problem you have identified or a problem that your students can identify. You can create games that can help students learn about the problem differently and participating students can submit their work directly to Google Classroom.

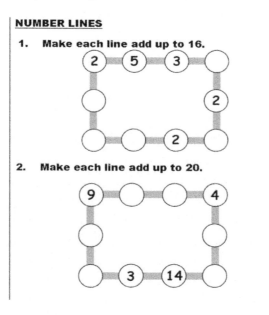

1. Link Interactive Simulations

There are several websites dedicated to providing helpful math simulations. Sites like Explore Learning have thousands of math simulations and math variations that students can look up to solve mathematical problems. You can link these URLs in your classroom either as part of an assignment or through an Announcement.

2. Link to Playsheets

Playsheets fall between gamification and GBL. Teachers can link up relevant Playsheets and give these assignments to the students. These playsheets give immediate feedback to students, and it is an excellent learning and motivational tool that tells the students that they are on the right track.

3. Use Google Draw

Google Draw is another creative tool that allows students and teachers to create virtual manipulations such as charts, Algebra tiles, and so on. Draw images that make it easy for students to identify with Math. This can be used to create differentiated assignments targeting students with different learning levels.

4. Use digital tools

Digital tools such as Desmos, Geogebra, and Daum Equation Editor can also be used to solve various math problems. These tools can be used from Google Drive and integrated with other Google documents. Once done, students can submit their solved problems to Google Classroom.

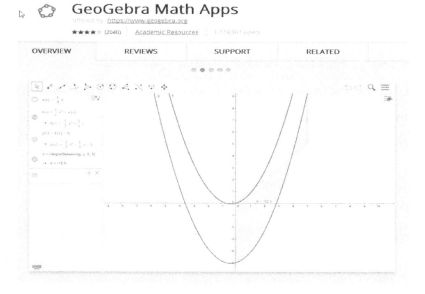

Teach programming

Get students to use programs such as Scratch or Google Apps Script that can enable them to exhibit their understanding of mathematical concepts.

Teaching Science

1. Hangout with Experts

Get experts you are connected to in real life to talk about their experiences working in a science-related field to help students with their science-related subjects. You can use Google Hangouts to send questions the class has and link it to your Google Classroom. This enables the students to access the Hangout and participate in the questioning or even watch the interview after the session is done. The Hangout Session can be archived for later viewing.

2. Collecting Evidence

Have your students submit 'evidence' of science experiments by sending in photos or videos of their science projects and uploading it to Google Classroom.

3. Give Real life examples

Tailor-made your science projects and assignments so that it gets students to go outside and get real-life samples which they can record on their mobile devices. They can take these images and submit it immediately to the Google Classroom. Make it interesting, students that submit their answers faster get extra points!

4. Crowdsourcing information

Get students into the whole idea and activity of crowdsourcing. Create a Google Spreadsheet with a specific topic and specify what information they need and what goals the project needs to accomplish. Upload the document to Google Classroom and get students to find and contribute information.

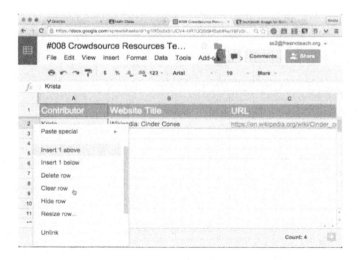

Teaching Writing & Reading

1. Provide Templates

Allow students to access writing templates on Google Classroom for things such as formal letters, informal letters, report writing, assignment templates, resumes, and cover letter formats.

2. Reading Records

Establish a weekly reading record on Google Classroom where they can record information on the times that they have read during the week. So instead of writing it down on a reading diary, allow them to update a form on Google Classroom by entering the necessary data. This allows them to immediately add in the information of the books that they have read while it is still fresh in their minds.

Class Reading Record
Tom Barrett
ICT in my Classroom - http://tbarrett.edublogs.org

Name

Date

Book Title

Page Numbers

Comments
What did you enjoy? Did you struggle with any words? What help did you get?

I read with...

Submit

3. Collaborate on Writing Projects

Get your students to collaborate on writing projects via Group assignments. These projects can be anything from preparing newspaper articles, journals, e-portfolios, and so on.

4. Spelling Tests

You can create a simple 1-10 or 1-20 weekly spelling test via Google Form. Get students to type in their answers as you read out the list of words. Once completed, apply a formula to judge if they are correct or not, and it becomes self-marking.

Spelling Test

Tom Barrett
ICT in my Classroom - http://tbarrett.edublogs.org

Name

1)

2)

3)

4)

5)

6)

8)

Teaching Physical Education

Didn't think PE could be done via Google Classroom? Here are some ideas:

1. Post Fitness Videos

Post fitness videos to help your students understand how to perform a workout. Send out videos to any psychical activity that you want students to conduct on their next PE session, or you can also just post a video after classes so students can practice the exercise in their own time and work on their form.

2. Get students to post videos of their daily workout

Have your students post videos in the public feed on your Google Classroom with a hashtag such as #midweekfitspo. Encourage students to work out and post their videos each week.

3. Link to safety videos

Post up safety videos for your PE activities, so your students know what kind of skills they need to follow to exercise safely.

4. Post Resources for activities

PE teachers can also post useful resources for games and activities ahead of time such as rules and method of playing before the student's next PE session. It would help the students prepare and know what to expect for their next class.

5. Create a Fitness Tracker

Assign students to a Fitness Tracker spreadsheet and make a copy for each student. Assign a due date for the end of the semester for their physical education class. You can monitor each student's progress by checking out the assignment folder in the Google Classroom.

Use the spreadsheet to get your students to track their progress. Whenever students update their results, the spreadsheet automatically updates to dynamic charts so students can see their progress visually over the entire semester.

You can either pair students up to work in partners or individually. Get the students to take photos of each other's forms when practicing certain tasks so that you can evaluate their form and correct it by way of giving them feedback via Classroom or during PE classes. A rubric would be helpful here too so that students can self-evaluate their own workouts and make corrections where necessary.

Other Teaching Methods to Use

1. Attach Patterns and Structures

Upload patterns and structures that students can identify and explain. Students can also collaborate with other students to identify patterns and structures to come up with solutions.

2. Use geometric concepts

Use Google Drawings or Slides to insert drawings of geometric figures for math, science, and even for art.

3. Collaborate online with other teachers

If you know other teachers have modules or projects which would come in handy with your class, collaborate together and enable your students to join in as well. Different teachers allow for different resources, and the teaching load can also be distributed.

4. Peer Tutoring

Senior students can also be allowed to access your Google Classroom at an agreed time on a weekly basis to tutor and give support to junior students or students in differentiated assignments.

5. Celebrate success

Google Classroom also enables the teacher to encourage students through comments whenever they submit an assignment because feedback can be given immediately and this can be done either privately or publicly.

6. Digital quizzes

Quizzes can be used for various subjects on Google Classroom. Get your students to submit their answers quickly for extra points.

7. Share presentations

Share presentations and slides with your students to help them with whatever assignments you have given them.

Chapter 9 Tips And Tricks To Get The Most Out Of Google Classroom

Both teachers and students can benefit from Google Classroom. It is an easy platform that brings together some of the best apps that Google has to offer to help teachers get the most out of their lectures and students to learn in new and exciting ways. Here we will look at some of the tips and tricks that both students and teachers can try to get the most out of the Google Classroom platform.

Tips for Teachers

Tip 1: Learn all the ways to give feedback.

Your students are going to thrive with as much feedback as you can provide them and Classroom offers you many options for this. You can leave comments on assignments that students' hand in, on the file that is submitted, through email, and so much more. Consider the best places to leave feedback and let your students know so they can be on the lookout for ways to improve.

Some of the ways that you can utilize comments include:

Class comments—you can do this by starting a common for the whole class on the outside of the assignment or in the announcement. This is going to be a comment that the whole class is going to see so don't use it if you just want to talk to the individual student. It is a good option to use if you want to answer a question that a lot of people have.

Private comments—you can do this by going into the file of an individual student. You will be able to see the submissions this student has made and can click on the comment bar near the bottom. When you add a comment, the student will be the only one who can see it.

Comments to media—you can do this by clicking on the file that the student submitted to you. Highlight the area and then comment on that particular part of the project. This can help you to show an example of the student or explain your thoughts and how something needs to be changed.

Tip 2: Use the description feature

When creating an assignment, make sure to add a nice long description. This is where you explain what the assignment is all about, how to complete it, and even when the assignment is due. Often students are juggling many classes all at once and by the time they get to the assignment, they have forgotten all the instructions you gave them in class. Or if a student missed class that day, the description can help them understand what they missed. A good description can help to limit emails with questions and can help students get started on the assignment without confusion.

Tip 3: Use Flubaroo

Grading can take up a lot of your time, especially when dealing with many students and multiple classes. You want to provide your students with accurate feedback as quickly as possible, but traditional teaching can make this impossible. Add-ons like Flubaroo can make this easier. When creating a quiz or test, you can use Flubaroo so that when a student submits their answers, the app will check them and provide a score right away. The student can see how well they did on the quiz and where they may need to make some changes.

This kind of add-on is best for things such as multiple choice assignments and tests. It allows the student to see what they understand right away without having to wait for the teacher to correct everything. You are able to go back and change the grade on a particular assignment if the add-on grades incorrectly, you want to add bonus points, or for some other reason.

If you are creating assignments like discussion posts, opinions, projects, and essays, Flubaroo is not the best option for you. This app is not going to understand how to grade these projects and since each one is more creative and doesn't necessarily have a right or wrong answer, it is important for the teacher to go in and grade. There are many places where you can provide feedback, even at various points of the project, to help the student make changes before the final grade.

Tip 4: Reuse some of your old posts

At times, you may have an assignment, question, or announcement that is similar to something you have posted before. For example, if you have a weekly reading or discussion assignment that is pretty much the same every week, you will be able to use the reuse option on Classroom. To do this, just click on the "+" button that is on the bottom right of the screen. You will then be able to select "Reuse post." Pick from a list of options that you already used for the class. If there are any modifications, such as a different due date, you can make those before posting again. When reusing the post, you have the option to create new copies of the attachments that were used in the original posting.

Tip 5: Share your links and resources

There may be times that you find an interesting document, video, or other media that you would like your students to see. Or they may need resources for an upcoming project, and you want to make it easier for them to find. In this case, you should use the announcement feature. This allows all the important documents to be listed right at the top of the classroom rather than potentially getting lost further down in assignments.

This is a great tip to use for items of interest that you would like to share with your students or for documents and files that they will need right away. If you have a resource that the students will need throughout the year, you should place it into the "About" tab to prevent it getting lost as the year goes on.

Tips for Students

Tip 1: Pick one email for all of your classes

Consider having a dedicated email that is for all of your classes. You don't need to separate it and have an email for each of your classes, but create a new email that will only accept information from all classes using Google Classroom. Whenever a teacher announces they use this platform, you will use this email. This helps you to keep all of your classes in one place and can prevent you from missing out on your announcements and assignments because they got lost in all your personal emails.

Tip 2: Check your classes daily

As the year goes on, your teacher will probably get into a routine of when they make posts, and you can check the class at that time. But it is still a good idea to stay on top of a class and check it each day. You never know when you may forget about an assignment that is almost due or when the teacher will add an extra announcement for the whole class. If you only check your classes on occasion, you could miss out on a lot of important information along the way. Check in daily to stay up to date and to get everything in on time.

Tip 3: Look at the calendar

One of the first places you should go when opening up to a class is the Calendar. This is going to list everything important that is coming your way in the next few months (updated as the teacher adds new announcements and assignments) so you can plan out your time. For some students, it is easier to get a grasp on the work when it is in table form rather than just looking at a date in the announcements. Use this as a planning tool and check it often to see if there is anything new to add to your schedule.

Tip 4: Ask questions for clarification

Classroom makes it easier for students to ask the questions they need before starting an assignment. In some classrooms, it can be hard to find time to ask a question. When twenty or more students are asking questions at the same time, or the teacher runs out of time and barely gets the assignment out before the next bell, there are many students who may leave the classroom without any clue how to begin on an assignment.

With Classroom, the students can ask any questions they have when it is convenient. If they have a question about an assignment, they can comment on the assignment or send an email. If they have a question about some feedback that is left for a test, discussion, or essay, they can ask it right on the assignment.

Tip 5: Learn about all the features of Google

Google has many great features that both students and teachers can take advantage of. Many people don't realize all of the different apps that are available on Google, and since these apps can be used together with Classroom and are free, it is important to take advantage of as many as possible. Some of the best Google products that can help with learning include:

Gmail—Gmail makes it easier for students and teachers to communicate about the class without sharing the information with other students.

Calendar—students will be able to see at a glance when important assignments, tests, and other information occurs in their class.

Drive—Drive is a great place to put all assignments, questions, and other documents that are needed to keep up in class. Teachers can place learning materials and assignments inside for the student to see and students can submit their assignments all in one place.

YouTube—students are used to spending time on YouTube, and teachers can use this to their advantage to find educational videos for their class. Students can either look at links that the teacher provides or search for their videos.

Docs—this program works similar to Microsoft Word, but since it is free, it can be nice for those students who don't already have Word at home. Students can write, edit, and make changes just like on regular documents and then submit back to the teacher.

Google Earth/Maps—explore the world around us with these two great features. Google Earth lets students learn more about the world by allowing them to look up different areas and see them from an actual satellite. Google Maps can help with Geography around the world or students can even create their Maps with this program.

Tip 6: Don't forget about tests and quizzes

Sometimes, a teacher may give you a few days to complete a test at home if there isn't enough time to do everything in the classroom. This gives you a bit of freedom to study for longer and fit the test around your schedule, but when a test isn't due right away, it is sometimes easy to forget about it. Make sure to watch your Calendar and set up announcements to remind yourself that an important assignment or test is due.

The issue with forgetting about some of these things is that with the right add-ons, the system may grade the test as incomplete or give you a zero (if the test is multiple choice). The teacher may be willing to go back in and fix the grade or extend the due date if you talk to them, but it is still better to just get the test done in the first place. This shows that you can adhere to deadlines and saves some time for your teacher.

Google Classroom may seem like a simple platform, but there is just so much that you can do with it both as a teacher and as a student. The options for learning, sending information back and forth, and all the organization and freedom now available in the classroom can make this an attractive choice for many schools.

Chapter 10 FAQS About Google Classroom

As a teacher, there are a lot of different options that you can use to make the most out of your classroom and you may be curious as to why Google Classroom is the best option to help you out. There are many questions that you may have that pertain to Google Classroom. Some of the questions that you may have about Google Classroom include:

Is it easy to get started with Google Classroom?

Yes, it is really easy to work with Google Classroom, but you do need to remember that it is necessary to have the Google Apps for Education and your domain needs to be verified.

How are Apps for Education and Classroom connected?

To keep things simple, Google Classroom is not able to work without the help of Google Apps for Education. While you are able to use the Apps for Education all on its own, you will find that using Google Classroom is going to help to make all of it organized and it is much easier to work with. With the help of both the Classroom and Apps working together, both the students and the teachers are able to access the spreadsheets, slideshows, and documents as well as other links without having to worry about attachments and more. Even giving and receiving assignments and grades are easier when these two are combined together.

In addition, there is the option to download the Classroom Mobile app, which will make it easier to access your classes whenever and wherever you would like. This is going to be great for students who are on the go and don't have time to always look through their laptop to see announcements. Even teachers are able to use this mobile app to help them get up assignments and announcements when they are on the go so they can concentrate on other tasks later on.

Does it cost to use Google Classroom?

One of the best things about using Google Classroom is that it is completely free. All you need is a bit of time to help get it all setup, but it will not include any out of pocket costs to make it work. You will have to wait about two weeks in the beginning for your application to be reviewed before you are able to use the class, so consider setting this up early to prevent issues with falling behind.

You will never have to pay for anything when you are using Google Classroom. If you run into a vendor who is asking for you to pay for Google Classroom, you should report them to Google. It is highly likely that this is a fake vendor so do not work with them or provide them with any of your payment information. Google Classroom is, and always will be, free for you to use.

Can I still use Classroom if it is disabled on my domain?

One of the nice things about working with Classroom is that even if it has been disabled on a certain domain, you are still able to use it. With that being said, there are going to be a few restrictions. While you may still be able to get access to a lot of the features, such as Google Drive, Google Docs, and Gmail, you may not be able to see some of the slides, docs, and sheets that were saved in the classroom. It is always best to have your domain turned on when you are working in Google Classroom because this ensures that you are able to use all of the features that are available through the Classroom.

Do I need to have Gmail enabled to use classroom?

It is not necessary to have Gmail enabled in order to use the Google Classroom. You are able to use the Classroom as much as you would like without enabling Gmail, but you would find that you wouldn't be able to receive notifications if the Gmail account isn't turned on. If you would like to have some notifications sent to you, you need to have Gmail enabled.

If you are not that fond of using the Gmail account for this, it is possible to set up your own email server to make it work. This way, you will still be able to receive the notifications that are needed from the Classroom while using the email server that you like the most.

Will I have to work with ads on Google Classroom?

Many people like to work with Google Classroom because they don't have to worry about seeing ads all over the place. Classroom was designed for educational purposes, and Google recognizes that people don't want to have to fight with ads all of the time when they are learning. You can rest assured that Google and Classroom are not going to take your information and use it for advertising. This is part of the privacy and security that is offered with Google Classroom, which will protect both the student and the teacher from any phishing or spam.

If I have a disability, am I able to use Google Classroom?

Yes, those with disabilities are able to use Google Classroom. Some of the features are not yet complete, but Google is working to make some improvements to classroom so that those who have disabilities can use it too. Aside from using the Screen reader, there are a few other features that you can use with Android including:

BrailleBack: this is a great feature that is going to allow for Braille to be displayed on the Android Device, as long as you have your Bluetooth installed. This is also going to work with the Screen Reader feature that we talked about before. With this feature, you will also be able to input your text while interacting with your Android device.

Switch Access: it is also possible for you to use Switch Access, which is a tool that allows you to control your device with two or more switches. This is great for those who are dealing with limited mobility. It is also a good way to get notifications and alerts.

You are also able to tweak some of the settings that are in Google Classroom in regards to color correction, magnification, captions, touch and hold, using a speaking password, and more.

As you can see, there are a lot of neat things that you are able to do when it comes to using Google Classroom and it is pretty easy for everyone to be able to use. If you ever have some other questions about Google Classroom, you can always contact their support to get the assistance that you need.

Chapter 11 Guidelines & Suggestions for Classroom Management and Instructional Forms

Google Classroom allows you to extend the blended learning experience in a variety of ways; teachers can create excellent number of ways to enhance a student's grasp of school subjects and increase learning capabilities. The possibilities are endless where Google is concerned.

Google's biggest asset is its simplicity and ease of use. Using the various Google applications doesn't require a textbook to learn it, as with Google Classroom, all other apps are simple to set up, quick to learn and saves time and energy to get things done and organize your various files and documents. We will share ten best practices for Google Classroom that you can employ, to fully make use and take advantage of this pioneering online education tool.

1. Reduce the carbon footprints of your class

The idea of Google Classroom is to make things easier for teachers and students alike when learning things. It takes the conventional classroom and places it on the online sphere and enables students and educators to create spreadsheets and presentations, online documents and it makes sharing and communicating easier. Creating and sharing things digitally eliminates the need to printing. Schools use a lot of papers but utilizing Classroom enables you to remove the necessity of paper for simple things. Have an assignment? Save some trees, time and money by creating them on Classroom, distributing it to your students in your Classroom.

2.   Distribute and Collect Student's homework easily

The whole point of creating the assignments via Google Classroom is so that you can distribute it and collect the assignments quickly. Yes, you can say that you could get it done via email too. But Classroom's enable all these things to be done in one place. You'll know who has sent an assignment, who have passed their deadline and who needs more help with their work. It's all about lessening the hassle in your life.

3.   Utilizing the feedback function

With instant access, teachers are able to clarify doubts, concerns and misconceptions their students may have by providing feedback as and when students need it. As teachers, you eliminate possible issues that might arise while students are doing their assignments. This reduces the headache you might have upon receiving the assignments that don't meet the requirements. Assignments that are handed in that have issues can be immediately rectified as well, through private one-on-one feedback with the relevant student.

4.   Create your personalized learning environment

The main benefit of Google Classroom is the freedom that it gives teachers. Very often, teachers are required to follow the national syllabus forwarded by the Department or Ministry of Education in a country. While this is rightly done for the sake of uniformity and to ensure students across the country have access to the same level of education, utilizing Classroom, on the other hand, gives teachers the freedom to add and create a different environment for learning.

Teachers can focus on using different materials, subjects, and cater to the different levels and needs of students. If you are using Google Classroom, then make sure you use this aspect to your fullest advantage. You would be able to endorse a personalized learning system by giving your students different learning preferences such as choices of submitting answers, various types of online assignments and using online resources.

5.   Encourage real world applications

Encourage students to submit their assignments using real world material whether it's a series of videos or photos, a compilation of multimedia applications, using the many different apps out there to create amazing online presentations are just some of the things that students can do that will increase their learning tendencies and spark online discussions within the Classroom. This enables the students to apply and implement assignments that they have done in their real lives.

6.   Allow shy students to participate

As teachers, we know which students are more extrovert that the other. Sometimes in conventional classroom settings, the shy kid or the kid with self-esteem issues or those that lack confidence have problems participating in classroom activities, speaking out or even raising their hand to answer questions. Google Classroom gives a safety barrier for students that fall into this category but allowing them to be more open with discussing and expressing themselves. As the teacher, you can also find creative ways to encourage these students to open up via game-based learning to promote trust, openness, teamwork, and collaboration.

7. Allow for coaching

Some students need more coaching and a little bit more explanation. If you know some students in your class that needs it, you can give them extra instructions by privately messaging them. You can always follow up with them while they are doing their assignments just to check if they are on the right track. Additionally, you can also invite another teacher to collaborate and help with coaching your students.

8. Interactive Activities Using Google Classroom

The more and more you use Google Classrooms, the more you will be able to use Classrooms in many more ways than just connecting with your students and creating assignments.

Google Classroom, combined with other Google products such as Google Slides can really deliver powerful interactive user experiences and deliver engaging and valuable content.

Teachers looking to create engaging experiences in Google Classroom can use Google Slides and other tools in the Google suite of products to create unique experiences.

Here are some exciting ways that you can use Google Classroom and Google Slides to create an engaging learning experience for your students:

1.   Create eBooks via PDF

PDF files are so versatile and you can open them in any kind of device. Want to distribute information only for read-only purposes? Create a PDF! You can use Google Docs or even Google Slides for this purpose and then save it as a PDF document before sending it out to your classroom.

2.   Create a slide deck book

Make your textbooks paperless too, not just assignments. Teachers can derive engaging and interactive content from the web and include it in the slide deck books, upload it to the Google Classroom and allow your students to access them. Make sure to keep it as read only.

3.   Play Jeopardy

This method has been used in plenty of Google Classroom and the idea was created by Eric Curts, a Google Certified Innovator, created this template that you can copy into your own Google Drive to customize with your own questions and answers. Scores can be kept on another slide that only you can control.

4.   Create Game-Show Style Review Games

Another creative teacher came up with a Google Slide of 'Who Wants to be a Millionaire?'. The template allows you to add in your questions and get students to enter the answers in the text box. Again, you keep the score!

5. Use Animation

Did you know you can create animations in your Google Slide and share in on Classroom? This tutorial shows you how. You can also encourage your students to create animation to explain their assignments. This is really making them push boundaries and think out of the box.

6. Create stories sand adventures

Using Google Slides and uploading them to Google Classroom to tell a story. Turn a question into a story and teach your students to create an adventure to describe their decision for the outcome of the character in their story. The stories can be a certain path that the students have chosen for the character or a story that explains the process of finding a solution.

7. Using Flash Cards

Flash cards are great ways to increase the ability to understand a subject or topic. Do you want to create an interactive session on Google Classroom using flash cards? You can start by utilizing Google Sheets which gives you a graphic display of words and questions and then to reveal the answers, all you need to do is click. Compared to paper flash cards, these digital flash cards allow you to easily change the questions, colors as well as the answers of the cards depending on what you are teaching the class. Digital flash cards also are an interactive presentation method that is guaranteed to engage your Classroom and bring about a new way of teaching using Google Classroom's digital space.

Make vocabulary lessons, geography lessons and even history lessons fund and entertaining with digital flash cards.

8.   Host an online viewing party

Get your students to connect to Classroom at a pre-determined date and time when there is a noteworthy performance, play or even movie that is related to the subjects you are teaching in your class. Let them view the video together and also interact with them by adding questions to your Google Classroom and allowing your students to reply to you in real time. This way, you can see assess them on their reflections, level of understanding and their observations. You can also give your own interpretation of the scene and explain it again to students who do not quite understand.

There is no limit to what a teacher can do with Google Classroom and the entire Google suite of apps whether its Google Slides or Google Calendar or even Google Maps. The only thing you would need is creativity and the desire to give your student a different experience when using Google Classroom.

Chapter 12 Other Ways Google Classroom Can Help You Succeed

Google Forms

One of the features that you can do with Google Classroom is to use the Google Forms. These make it really easy for the teacher to obtain information from their students and for the students to leave some feedback about assignments, the class and more. To keep this simple, the teacher would be able to set up a Google Form in order to open up responses from people in the class. They can ask some open-ended questions, send out a survey, or something else. When the student is done with the survey, it will be marked as complete so the teacher knows when the information is all complete.

Many times the teacher will use this as a way to provide their students with a survey at the end of the year. They can ask how the class worked, what things, if any, they would change, and so on. This is a great way for teachers to keep up with what is going on in their classrooms and to see if the work is really being that effective.

Google Calendar

The Google Calendar is all automated on the system so this makes it easier for students and teachers to keep track of the things that they need to work on when they are in a particular class. Whenever a teacher puts up a new assignment, project, test or another thing for the students to work on, the due date is automatically going to be placed and synced up with the Google Calendar. Students can easily go through and see when their assignments are due for all of their classes without having to search through all of the classes or spend a lot of time wondering when it is all due. The student also has the option to choose to sync together the dates that are on their Calendar with their email accounts or even with their mobile phones so they can get notifications when they are approaching a due date.

Use the About Page

One thing that a lot of students will forget to use is the About Page because they don't think that it is all that important for them. But filling out this About Page can be really good for everyone involved. For the teacher, it is a good idea to fill in the About Page with accurate information to help the student understand what class they are taking and who the teacher is. For example, the teacher may want to consider writing a good description of the particular class as well as links to your website, a little bit about you, and some of your contact information in case a student needs to get ahold of you.

In addition, your students can also go through and fill out an About Page as well. They can tell a little bit about themselves to introduce themselves to the other people in the class, share their interests, and so on. Teachers could choose to make this one of the assignments for the students to be a kind of ice breaker and to help them to learn a bit more about the students.

Reuse the posts

One of the nice things that a teacher will be able to do with Google Classroom is that they can take some of the posts that they used before, in another class or in a previous class, and then reuse them a bit. This can be announcements, assignments, and even questions from their previous classes to help them keep up with the work, especially if the information still works with this current class.

For the students, it is possible to go through and see some of the old classes that they were in. This can be helpful if you need to review something that is inside of the older class or you want to get ahold of some papers or discussions that you want to use from a past semester. You just need to go through some of your past archived classes to find what you would like.

Setting the theme

Some students go into their Google Classroom and leave everything the way that it is. They are happy with the theme and how everything is set up so they won't want to switch anything around. But if you would like to take your Google Classroom and set it up in order to have some personalization to it, you will be able to do that by changing some of the settings inside of Google Classroom. There are many different color palettes that you are able to choose from as well as different themes so you can mess around with this a little bit to find what works the best for your account. In order to set up a new theme that you want to use in the classroom, you can use the following steps:

- Open up Class
- From here, you can select the Theme button that is at the bottom of the image in your image settings.
- Now you can either select an image from the gallery or you can click on the Patterns button in order to pick out the theme that you would like.
- Once you have picked out what you would like to have there, you can click on Apply and the new theme is going to be all set up.

It is also possible to upload some of your own pictures to the gallery in order to use that when picking out the new theme that you are using.

Find conversation starters

This is one that the teacher is most likely going to work with, but as a student, you will be able to go through and see what conversation starters the teacher has posted for you. You should be on the lookout for these to see what the teacher is asking for, such as feedback on the recent announcements or even information about the discussion groups that you need to respond to for a grade. This is a fantastic way for you to keep everyone in the class united, even if they are all in different locations.

Send out emails

Since this is a Google program, you will be able to use the Gmail account to send out emails to other people in the class. The teacher will be able to choose whether to send out an email to individual students if they need to, or they can pick out groups of students that they need to share information with, such as new announcements for the whole class.

In addition, the students would be able to use the email system to talk to others inside of their Google Classroom. For example, if they need to ask the teacher a question and they don't want to post it on the open forum or discussion, they are able to send out an email to do this. They can also use their email to talk to individual students or to groups of students who are in the same classroom as well.

Check progress

While the student is working on the project the teacher will be able to check how well the student is doing simply by clicking on the Submission History. They can then go from here and click on Assignment Status to check the history to see whether or not the student has been following the guidelines that were set for the assignment or if the work is just sitting there. It helps the teachers to keep track on who is getting the work done and who may need a little bit of encouragement and can hold some of the students accountable.

This is also a good way for the teacher to determine if they need to provide some extra assistance to their students or not. If they notice that someone has been logging in and doing the work but they are not getting very far, they may be able to come in and see if the student needs a little bit of extra help with the assignment or not. This is a great way to provide some individual help to the student, something that would be almost impossible for the teacher to do in the traditional classroom.

There are so many different things that you will be able to do when you are working with Google Classroom. It has some great features that are perfect for both the student and for the teachers as well, which is why this is one of the top reasons that Google Classroom is one of the best in the industry. Learn how to use the various features that are available with Google Classroom, and you are going to see some great changes in the way that students learn and teachers teach in no time.

Chapter 13 Pros And Cons Of Using Google Classroom In eLearning

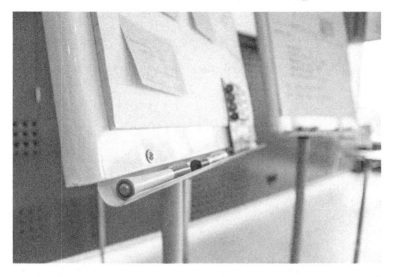

Google Classroom was presented about four years prior and has been developing quickly from that point forward. Google has reinforced its instruction assets and, therefore, the greater part of K–12 understudies across the country use in any event one of its items.

Google Classroom is a web-based learning the executives framework intended for schools. It reflects the day by day administrative work, correspondence and record-keeping assignments we do disconnect. With Google Classroom, you can impart archives and assets to understudies, give input, and allocate and gather work. Classes are private and secret key ensured, and posts must be seen by individual class individuals. Further more's, sans everything.

Sounds extraordinary, correct? However the amazing stage causes worries for certain instructors. How about we analyze a portion of the advantages and disadvantages of utilizing Google Classroom.

On the positive side, Google Classroom's record sharing, information assortment, correspondence channels and shut condition are incredible benefits. It's anything but difficult to begin a classroom — accommodating directions manage you through the whole procedure. When you include understudies, sharing is considerably simpler; you simply send assets to the whole class.

Something I've constantly refreshing about Google applications is that you make a repository of work — exercise plans, assignments, interchanges, grade records, and so on — that you can reuse. It's likewise pleasant to diminish paper use and not need to complain with a whimsical scanner.

The work accommodation process is compelling, as well. You can make a task, report a due date and send singular duplicates to every understudy. At the point when understudies total work, they "turn it in" and it's naturally imparted to you. No more gifts to sort. Not any more tendinitis from carrying packs of understudy work.

Criticism is the superpower of Google Classroom. Remarking can happen at each progression of a task. At the point when you allocate work, understudies can likewise post questions. Those hesitant to talk in class can in any case solicit help on the web. You can remark on works-in-progress, giving assistance en route. Input on finished work can be a two-way discussion, reflecting an in-class meeting. Not any more unintelligible edge takes note of that understudies overlook.

Presently, we should take a gander at a portion of the cons.

Classroom arrangement might be simple; however you have to make special records for each understudy. As of now have an individual Gmail account? Indeed, you can't utilize it here. So as to keep a classroom totally private, you should make new records, including for yourself, through the Google Classroom area. This may mean recalling — or overlooking — new passwords.

Because of the encased and private condition, it's troublesome or difficult to impart items to the more extensive school community, the general population or guardians — regardless of whether you need to. (Classroom schedules with due dates and occasions are open, however.)

In spite of the fact that it records understudy grades, Google Classroom doesn't contain an undeniable evaluation book. You can send out Google Sheets to all-inclusive database documents good with other evaluation book applications, however it's an extra, unwieldy advance.

The inescapability of Google Classroom flashes significant inquiries regarding security and promoting. Google has prevailing with regards to making new, youthful clients who will probably stay faithful to its image. Because Google brings in cash from web-based publicizing, it's imperative to consider how and when understudies are affected while utilizing its foundation.

Google Classroom Review: 16 Pros And Cons Of Using Google Classroom In eLearning

How might you want to be a piece of a classroom center point where you could speak with your students, furnish them with useful input at whatever point they required it, and streamline the sharing of classroom archives and assignments? Google Classroom does precisely that; it is Google's ambitious addition to online instruction too to the Learning Management System industry, and it expects to make classrooms everywhere throughout the world paperless, yet additionally increasingly viable. Google Classroom is accessible through Google Apps for Education, as right now it is focused on scholarly institutions just, and not corporate preparing. Right now, share a Google Classroom survey by referencing 8 preferences and 8 detriments, so as to assist you with choosing whether Google Classroom is suitable for your eLearning courses.

8 Google Classroom Advantages

Simple to utilize and available from all gadgets.

Regardless of whether you are not a Google client, utilizing Google Classroom is easy. Aside from being conveyed through the Chrome program, which makes it open from all PCs, cell phones, and tablets, it makes it extremely simple for you to include the same number of students as you like, make Google reports to oversee assignments and declarations, post YouTube recordings, include interfaces, or join documents from Google Drive. Students will discover it similarly simple to sign in, just as get and turn in assignments.

Compelling correspondence and sharing.

Probably the best bit of leeway of Google Classroom is Google Docs; these reports are spared on the web and imparted to a limitless number of individuals, so when you make a declaration or task utilizing a Google doc, your students can get to it quickly through their Google Drive, as long as you have imparted it to them. Besides, Google Docs are effectively sorted out and customized in Google Drive organizers. At the end of the day, you no longer need messages to share data; you simply make a record, share it with the same number of students as you need, and presto!

Accelerates the task procedure.

What about making a task and dispersing it with only a tick of a catch? Also, what about students turning in the finished task surprisingly fast? Task process has never been faster and increasingly viable, as in Google Classroom you can without much of a stretch check who has submitted their task and who is as yet taking a shot at it, just as offer your input right away.

Viable input.

Talking about input, Google Classroom offers you the chance to offer your online help to your students immediately; this implies criticism turns out to be progressively powerful, as crisp remarks and comments have greater effect on students' brains.

No requirement for paper.

There may be a day that evaluating papers would be difficult to envision; Google Classroom is surely keen on arriving at the earliest opportunity. By bringing together eLearning materials in a single cloud-based area, you can go paperless and quit agonizing over printing, giving out, or in any event, losing your students' work!

Clean and easy to use interface.

Remaining faithful to clean Google format guidelines, Google Classroom invites you to a domain where each and every structure detail is basic, intuitive, and easy to understand. Obviously, Google clients will feel right comfortable.

Incredible remarking framework.

Students can remark on explicit areas within pictures for an assortment of online courses. Moreover, you can make URLs for intriguing remarks and utilizing them for additional online conversation.

Is for everybody.

Instructors can likewise join Google Classroom as students, which implies that you can make a Google Classroom for you and your associates and use it for personnel gatherings, data sharing, or expert advancement.

8 Google Classroom Disadvantages

Troublesome record the board.

Google Classroom doesn't permit access from numerous areas. Moreover, you can't sign in with your own Gmail to enter it; you should be signed in Google Apps for Education. Subsequently, in the event that you have effectively an individual Google ID, it might be disappointing to shuffle various Google accounts. For instance, on the off chance that you have a Google report or a photograph in your Gmail and you need to share it in the Google Classroom, you should spare it independently in your PC's hard drive, log out, and afterward sign in again with your Google Classroom account. Quite an issue.

Limited incorporation alternatives.

Google Classroom hasn't yet incorporated with Google Calendar, or any schedule at all, which may mess some up with sorting out material and task cutoff times.

Too "googlish".

First time Google clients may get confounded, as there are a few catches with symbols recognizable just to Google clients. Additionally, despite improved coordination among Google and YouTube, which fundamentally helps video sharing, support for other mainstream devices isn't implicit, and you may think that its baffling that you should, for instance, convert a straightforward Word archive to a Google Doc to work with. All things considered, you will just get yourself agreeable in the Google Classroom condition as long as the instruments you are utilizing are lined up with Google administrations.

No computerized refreshes.

Activity feed doesn't refresh consequently, so students should invigorate consistently all together not to miss significant declarations.

Troublesome student sharing.

Students can't impart their work to their companions, except if they become "proprietors" of an archive, and, after its all said and done they should support sharing choices, which will make a confusion in the event that they need to impart a report to their, say, 50+ schoolmates.

Editing issues.

At the point when you make a task and you convey it to students, students become "proprietors" of the record and they are permitted to edit it. That implies that they can erase any piece of the task they need, which could cause issues, regardless of whether it happens coincidentally.

No mechanized tests and tests.

One of the primary reasons that Google Classroom can't yet completely supplant your Learning Management System is that it doesn't give mechanized tests and tests to your students. When all is said in done, Google Classroom is more suitable for a mixed learning experience than a completely online program.

Indifferent.

Talking about a mixed learning condition, Google Classroom has not coordinated Google Hangouts, which makes an issue; online association among instructors and students is just conceivable through Google records. Viable training requires communication and building associations with students, and online conversations are the most ideal approach to accomplish this in a virtual domain. Shockingly, it is extremely unlikely to have a live talk in Google Classroom; in any event, once more, not yet.

Since you know the favorable circumstances and hindrances of Google Classroom from this Google Classroom survey, you might be keen on find out about free eLearning assets.

Conclusion

Google Classroom has every chance of becoming a popular international online learning platform (some functions are currently in beta testing). Nowadays, when virtually all types of content is moving from analog, physical and static to digital, this is a great chance to make the education system as flexible and personalized as possible.

For NGOs, the service is interesting not only with a wide range of tools for work but also with its interactivity - boring manuals are a thing of the past!

Google Classroom is available wherever there is an Internet connection. The class can be accessed on a computer in any browser, as well as from mobile devices based on Android and Apple iOS.

Google Classroom can be used by people with complete or partial visual impairment - they have screen readers. For example, VoiceOver was created for iOS devices and TalkBack for Android.

Google cares about the security of the information space; there is no advertising in the Class, and no posted materials can be used for commercial purposes.

Made in the USA
Monee, IL
23 August 2020